Don't Pack Your Bags Yet!

Anita Oyakhilome

LoveWorld Publications

Don't Pack *Your Bags* Yet!

ISBN 978-35623-2-0

First Printing 2001

BELIEVERS' LOVEWORLD INC.
aka Christ Embassy

UNITED KINGDOM:
Christ Embassy Int'l Office
Suite 219 Estuary House
Ballards Road, Dagenham
Rm 10 9AB

P.O. Box 21520,
London E10 5FG
Tel: 0181-5172367

NIGERIA:
P.O. Box 13563,
Ikeja, Lagos.
Tel: 01-4934393

e-mail: cec@christembassy.org
website: www.christembassy.org

CONTENTS

Foreword

Sharing an apartment with friends or relatives might sound exciting and adventurous because it affords one the opportunity to get more acquainted with them. It opens doors for a rewarding fellowship and a wonderful experience of sharing together.

In a few cases, however, things may not turn out like they should. While some people have beautiful memories and testimonies of such moments in their lives, others have a contrary experience for several reasons. As both parties get to discover each other, one may get fed up; feel used and may not be able to tolerate the presence of the other anymore.

In other words, the relationship might become sour, leaving memories of sad moments, in spite of all the accomplished dreams, seasons of joy, laughter and happiness the friendship has accrued over the years.

Leaving home with dashed hopes and a desperate heart is definitely not a position in which one should be found. God always remains *"our ever present help"* **(Psalm 46:1).** Suppose your friend with whom you have lived for several years, comes home one day and says, *'Please, could you pick your bags and leave'*, then the question of what to do next or where to go might arise. Your landlord, your boss or your school might do the same, but God is saying to you today, *'Don't pack your bags yet, because I am not through with you.'* The Bible has proved several times that the God whom you serve, continually delivers you no matter how tough the situation you find yourself.

What's In Your Bag?

The bags you carry could contain the desires, visions and dreams you were about to give up. The Word of God says,

"So shall the knowledge of wisdom be unto thy soul: when thou hast found it, then there shall be a reward and thy expectation shall not be cut off."

(Proverbs 24:14)

Don't throw away your desires. God uses your strong desires to bring your dreams to pass. Write down your visions as God directed in **Habakkuk 2:2.** He says, *"...Write the vision, and make it plain upon tables, that he may run that readeth it."*

Some people give up too soon. Even when it comes to spiritual matters, they lose their confidence in the Word too easily. You can give up on physical things but don't ever give up on praying, studying and doing the Word of God. You must remind God of His promises because not one word of all His promises has ever failed. He is a faithful Father. The Word of God says,

"For as the rain cometh down, and the snow from heaven, and returneth not thither, but watereth the earth, and maketh it bring forth and bud, that it may give seed to the sower, and bread to the eater: "So shall my word be that goeth forth out of my mouth: it shall not return unto me void, but it shall accomplish that which I please, and it shall prosper in the thing whereto I sent it."
(Isaiah 55:10-11)

The Word of God to you will always work for you. No matter who demands that you leave; no matter what situation stretches you to give up, God wants you to know that His indwelling Presence remains in you wherever you go upon the face of the earth. He is definitely with you, working on your behalf. In fact, you might have to leave invariably, but it would of necessity turn out for the best, if you allow God to have full control. As long as God is in control of your life, you will move upward and forward only.

"Blessed be the Lord, who daily loadeth us with benefits, even the God of our salvation." **(Psalm 68:19)**

Every child of God is living to experience a daily outpour of God's blessing. It's a daily loading of benefits. Anyone can tell you to go away, but God would never tell you off. Instead He says,

"Come unto me, all ye that labour and are heavy laden, and I will give you rest.
"Take my yoke upon you, and learn of me; for I am meek and lowly in heart: and ye shall find rest unto your souls.
"For my yoke is easy, and my burden is light."

(Matthew 11:28-30)

Your desires and dreams may be the content of the bag you are carrying. It may be your broken relationships or even broken fellowship with God. God can restore broken relationships. Don't carry your heavy bag alone. Cast your heavy burden upon Him. Tell Him all about it and resign from all your worries and fears. Take up His rest - enter into His rest. Believe His Word completely for He is able to help you and sustain you, even in all your anxieties. Throw your dreams, challenges; your whole being into His ever-open arms.

Anita Oyakhilome

1

Why Me?

"Giving no offence in any thing, that the ministry be not blamed: But in all things approving ourselves as the ministers of God, in much patience, in afflictions, in necessities, in distresses, In stripes, in imprisonments, in tumults, in labours, in watchings, in fastings... As unknown, and yet well known; as dying, and, behold, we live; as chastened, and not killed; As sorrowful, yet always rejoicing; as poor, yet making many rich; as having nothing, and yet possessing all things." **(2 Corinthians 6:3-5,9,10)**

Many people assume turbulent times are not for Christians and that anyone in a tough situation might have offended God; especially when the situation is prolonged **(2 Timothy 3:12)**. This is far from the truth. Your road to accomplishing success will definitely have trials and challenges.

Jesus knew that we would encounter problems in this world, but He confirmed that as we remain in Him, we would live a life full of peace even in the face of them all. You must be of good cheer; rejoicing always because He has overcome the world and given you the place of victory!

"These things I have spoken unto you, that in me ye might have peace. In the world ye shall have tribulation: but be of good cheer; I have overcome the world." **(John 16:33)**

These words of the Master must re-echo in the heart of every believer if he must have a victorious experience in life. In this scripture is the assurance that we are not alone.

I want you to know that distressing situations come from the enemy - the devil, but God always has a victory plan for His children. You may wonder why God left us in this world of trials and temptations. In other words, you may want to know why He allows trials to come our way in life. These are referred to as *'the sufferings of this present time'* **(Romans 8:18-19)**. But you need to know that God has made His power available to us and lifted us over principalities and powers. Sometimes Satan wants us to feel guilty by asserting that our love for God is based on selfishness, because of all the benefits we enjoy as His children.

We don't serve God because we don't face challenges or trials neither do we serve God only because we want our problems solved, or because of what we want from Him. We do not serve God for any selfish motive and the devil is sad to know this. He is even more miserable for knowing that we are partakers of our Heavenly Father's nature and inheritance. This brings to mind the story of a rich man in the Bible called Job. He feared God and hated to do evil.

Job 1:8-9,

"And the LORD said unto Satan, Hast thou considered my servant Job, that there is none like him in the earth, a perfect and an upright man, one that feareth God, and escheweth evil?

"Then Satan answered the LORD, and said, Doth Job fear God for nought?"

God has confidence in His children. He believed so much in Job's integrity and love for Him that He challenged Satan with his wealth. Next time you find yourself in any challenging situation, rejoice because God is using you to boast to the devil and the cohorts of hell. He knows you are capable of handling any situation without your personality being tarnished or diminished.

"For which cause we faint not; but though our outward man perish, yet the inward man is renewed day by day. For our light affliction, which is but for a moment, worketh for us a far more exceeding and eternal weight of glory;"
(2 Corinthians 4:16-17)

I love this scripture. Our inward man is being renewed day by day. It's not renewed on its own, you take an action to renew the inward man. Someone might dislike you and curse you with bad words because you offended him. This is not a trial or a challenge. Those words were wasted because they can't affect you. The Bible says, *"Surely there is no enchantment against Jacob, neither is there any divination against Israel:.."* **(Number 23:23)** It's the words that proceed out of your mouth that count.

If you are going through a tough time, it's time to change what you see and how you interpret your situation. Now change your confession to *"I am yielding a multiplied harvest of what I have sown, it is getting better every day. Glory to God."* How do you see yourself? I would like you to observe Paul's situation and his declarations.

"By pureness, by knowledge, by longsuffering, by kindness, by the Holy Ghost, by love unfeigned, By the word of truth, by the power of God, by the armour of righteousness on the right hand and on the left, By honour and dishonour, by evil report and good report: as deceivers and yet true; As unknown, and yet well known; as dying, and, behold, we live; as chastened, and not killed; As sorrowful, yet always rejoicing; as poor, yet making many rich; as having nothing, and yet possessing all things." **(2 Corinthians 6:6 -10)**

These words of Apostle Paul are mind-blowing. He describes the transforming power of the Word of God on us: as sorrowful yet *always* rejoicing; as having nothing, and yet possessing all things.

Whatever you ponder on controls you. That's why you must be mindful of what you brood upon. Think the thoughts of God. Think the Word of God. You can make yourself happy. It depends on the character of your thoughts. Whatever you think of at this moment can change the expression on your face.

Now, the question is why are some Christians suffering? The answer can be easily seen in the scriptures. God said, *"my people perish for lack of knowledge"* **(Hosea 4:6).** Christians suffer in extreme ignorance because they lack the knowledge and application of God's Word. Some are too shy to testify of God's divine intervention. Inspite of answers to their prayers: healing miracles; a lump disappearing, breast cancer being healed, promotion at their work place; they find it difficult to testify openly. They would rather keep it to themselves.

Some people suffer because they've not learnt to declare God's Word. They rather confess their situation or condition. Some suffer because they are silent. Some are too lazy to pray. They can see a boil on their forehead and instead of saying, *'In Jesus' Name I command this boil to leave this body right now'*, they say, *'I have a boil on my head and it's hurting me'.*

The devil is in charge of the world's system. This should reveal to you the origin of sickness and disease. But you are not of this world; you're from the glorious kingdom - the heavenly

Jerusalem. Just speak to whatever ailment is in your body; command it to die and pass out of your body. The words you speak are not your words; they're the words of your Father. This is the same word that created the universe and everything in the world responds to it.

Victors Translates Trial As Challenges

So many things happen to us in life. But the way we interprete them determines our response to them. The full knowledge of our identity is very important. When the Bible says that you are more than a conqueror, it infers that you cannot be defeated. No force can throw you off balance. Only victors translate problems into challenges. The right attitude is very vital for dynamic Christian living: this cannot be over-emphasized particularly in trying times.

Some folks act amoebic in the face of trial in their lives. They change their confessions and lifestyles to create *'adaptive features'* for the time being. They change from *'My God shall supply all my needs according to His riches in glory…'* to *'As the Lord provides…'* or worse still, *'We are managing…'*

They forget the ways of the Lord and all His goodness and opt for a lukewarm lifestyle - they are neither in the world nor in the Church. Nonetheless, things never get better for them, because their life is not consistent with the Word.

Your consistency in the profession of your faith is one of the most essential Christian attitudes towards dynamic living. Remain unshakeable in speaking God's Word, no matter what you see or how disastrous the situation may seem.

God's Word is any statement or message that is consistent with the plans, purpose and provisions of God. You must be wise to walk with a consciousness of your identity. You must find out what God says about you and the (temporary) circumstance you are facing. Then begin to speak the mind of God to yourself concerning the seemingly *'dead'* case. Keep speaking and doing God's word and every anomaly in your life will be put in check; in conformity to God's Word.

***"Then he answered and spake unto me, saying This is the word of the LORD unto Ze-rub-babel, saying, Not by might, nor by power, but by my spirit, saith the LORD of hosts."* (Zechariah 4:6)**

"But the Comforter, which is the Holy Ghost,

***whom the Father will send in my name, he shall teach you all things, and bring all things to your remembrance, whatsoever I have said unto you."*(John 14:26)**

Your life is not a loose web of events and circumstances. God has very specific plans for you, so you must pay attention to Him. Always look inward for the answer. When you rely completely on the enabling power of the Holy Ghost, He will calmly and gently guide you. He will provide you with excellent ideas and give you simple but specific instructions with calm confidence. Do them. They will yield excellent results and you will see that *every challenge you face is a springboard to greater heights.*

***"Have not I commanded thee? Be strong and of a good courage; be not afraid, neither be thou dismayed: for the LORD thy God is with thee whithersoever thou goest."* (Joshua 1:9)**

You must put this scripture to remembrance; your God is with you anytime and anywhere you go. Countless times in the Bible, we see God encouraging His people to be strong and courageous. This is the essence: the knowledge of

God's Word produces boldness, which leaves the devil trembling. When God commanded Joshua to be bold and courageous, Joshua in essence became all that it takes to be all that God said. By accepting God's Word, he became the bold and the strong and he surmounted every obstacle on his way to possessing the Promised Land. The Spirit of God's strength resides in all believers causing them to do great exploits in all life situations.

Trials: Why Not You?

Be disciplined; be strong. Don't run from pillar to post at the face of a trial. A tree has to be prunned for it to produce bountifully. Don't be afraid of trials or challenges. Don't ask *'Why me?'* Why not you? Your heavenly Father did not leave you without a defense. God expects you to operate by the principles of His kingdom and overcome. The anointing upon us destroys the yoke **(Isaiah 10:27)**. Therefore no believer should channel his hope on his ability alone, for it is not by might nor by power but by the Spirit of the living God.

"Every branch in me that beareth not fruit he taketh away: and every branch that beareth fruit, he purgeth it, that it may bring forth more fruit." **(John 15:2)**

"Thou therefore endure hardness, as a good soldier of Jesus Christ. No man that warreth entangleth himself with the affairs of this life; that he may please him who hath chosen him to be a soldier." **(2 Timothy 2:3-4)**

You need to be disciplined. You need to endure hardness. Don't chicken out when these light afflictions come on the scene, bearing in mind that they are only for a moment. Keep your gaze on the word, and on the Lord who has counted you faithful and enlisted you into His great victorious army.

"Thou wilt shew me the path of life: in thy presence is fulness of joy; at thy right hand there are pleasures for evermore." **(Psalm 16:11)**

Joy is the fruit of the recreated human spirit. God's joy in you is not dependent on circumstances. So you must live with a joyful heart always. Never allow any challenge weigh you down.

Remember that whatever challenges you face, are for a moment.

***"A merry heart doeth good like a medicine: but a broken spirit drieth the bones."*(Proverbs 17:22)**

***"All the days of the afflicted are evil: but he that is of a merry heart hath a continual feast."* (Proverbs 15:15)**

A joyful heart brings good health. A joyful heart is the spirit of a victor. He is not weighed down by light afflictions because he believes that God is able to take him through victoriously. Give no room for sorrow. God's power is easily activated on your behalf when you lead a cheerful lifestyle. You carry around you an atmosphere of miracles, as you live a joyful life.

Your strength is expressed by your laughter over issues that could have brought you down or in hours that could have been the darkest in your life. This is the way to live the victorious lifestyle. Never forget that the joy of the Lord is your strength **(Nehemiah 8:10).**

2

Crown Beyond Crisis

***"There is a vital force in man-the spirit of intelligence- and the inspiration of the Almighty giveth him understanding."* (Job 32:8 ~ The Amplified Translations)**

Many people started things they did not finish: great projects, buildings uncompleted, education without graduation, jobs that did not continue, plans that were never executed and so on. Some started well but ended badly. In other words, instead of making progress, their condition deteriorated. This is common with people whose lives are out of control. Peradventure, born again, Spirit-filled Christians are found in this category, it simply means they have not truly come to realise their place and possession in Christ. They suffer from an *'Identity Crisis!'* The devil takes advantage of such people who don't know their identity in Christ; who don't know who they are, what their rights are and what they can do in Christ. God never writes a man off, He only prepares men for the different stages of life. As the Psalmist revealed,

"For thou, O God hast proved us: thou hast tried us, as silver is tried. Thou broughtest us into the net; thou laidst afflictions upon our loins. Thou hast caused men to ride over our heads; we went through fire and through water; but thou broughtest us out into a wealthy place." **(Psalm 66:10-12)**

The Psalmist here refers to how God uses the trying times in our lives to purify us as silver. He highlights on the refining stages: *These refining stages are points when you put an end to to complaining, announcing your problems and doing nothing about it, the point when you stop feeling sorry for yourself, blaming people for your mistakes, when you stop feeling you cannot be trusted or seen as unreliable.* This refining stage is a process, when you deliberately decide to make changes. Just as you sit for an examination and after being certified *'passed'*, you expect a promotion, in the same way every appearance of a trial depicts an imminent promotion in your life. If you're passing through any trying time at the moment, rejoice for your promotion is just ahead.

Sometimes, we are tempted to follow another direction. As long as we are in this world, we will be tempted; there will always be a challenge for every believer in this world but Christ has given us power over all things.

We can cite a beautiful example from the book of Daniel. Some reporters, who found out that three Jews refused to bow down to the image had come to report to the king. These Jews were reputable men set over the affairs of Babylon and therefore would be expected by the king to obey his order. Rather they acted on the contrary. So, the king commanded the mightiest men that were in his army to bind Meshach, Shadrach and Abednego and cast them into the burning fiery furnace. These men were then bound and cast into the midst of the burning fiery furnace.

I want you to note that due to the intensity of the heat of the furnace, the men who threw these Jews into the furnace were slain by the flame. Yet Nebuchadnezzar the king did not repent. All of a sudden, he saw something marvelous in the midst of the furnace and he became astounded. He couldn't contain himself any longer so, he rose up in haste and asked his counselors,

"...Did not we cast three men bound into the midst of the fire? They answered and said unto the king, True O king.
"He answered and said lo, I see four men loose walking in the midst of the fire and they have no hurt and the form of the fourth is like the Son of God." **(Daniel 3:24-25)**

Then Nebuchadnezzar came near to the mouth of the burning fiery furnace and called Shadrach, Meshach and Abednego out of the furnace. The king called them the servants of the Most High God. He believed completely in their God when he saw the fourth man in the fire. Let's see his declaration of faith, as he poured his heart loud to God,

"...Blessed be the God of Shadrach, Meshach and Abednego, who hath sent his angel (of His presence), and delivered his servants that trusted in him, and have changed the king's word and yielded their bodies, that they might not serve nor wor-

ship any god, except their own God.

" Therefore, I make a decree, That every people, nation, and language, which speak any thing amiss against the God of Shadrach, Meshach and Abednego, shall be cut in pieces, and their houses shall be made a dunghill: <u>because there is no other God that can deliver after this sort.</u>

"Then, the king promoted Shadrach, Meshach and Abednego, in the province of Babylon." **(Daniel 3:28-30 paraphrased)**

This is a wonderful testimony. The Presence of Jesus is with you, whatever you might be going through . The Holy Ghost, who is the carrier of the divine Person of Christ, is in you. You are not alone.

Meshach, Shadrach and Abednego were promoted by the king after being proved by God. We can see how a whole nation of idolaters can be turned to God by our faith exercised in God in trying times.

God did not create us to manipulate us. He created us for a purpose. We have a Companion, who is the Comforter - The Holy Spirit. The promise that Christ made to us has been fulfilled. Jesus is seated on the right hand of the Father but the

Holy Spirit is here on earth with us. The Fourth Man is with you. He is also in you. Get rid of that long face, you can be happy today!

***"Seeing ye have purified your souls in obeying the truth through the Spirit unto unfeigned love of the brethren, see that ye love one another with a pure heart fervently: Being born again, not of corruptible seed, but of incorruptible, by the word of God, which liveth and abideth for ever"* (1 Peter 1:22-23).**

You are born of an incorruptible seed. God wants to prove that a new race, one that is indestructible, has emerged; a race that cannot be tarnished.

You are full of God's life. It's the life that cannot be conquered; the kind which even the grave cannot hold. It's the kind of life that controls situations and circumstances; one that dominates sin, sicknesses and diseases. This life is in you. The same Spirit that raised up Jesus Christ from the dead dwells in you; there's no spiritual force strong enough to destroy you, because the life that's within you is the incorruptible life of God!

3

Relationships

Every new creation in Christ is a peculiar person. If you are born again, you are not ordinary. Ordinary people regard themselves as common; the masses. They have no voice, no face and no identity. They are hidden in the crowd, carrying a frown with worry wrinkles and no confidence in themselves, or anyone. They speak empty words; they are at war with everyone. They like no one, including themselves. They have an identity crisis.

Ordinary people are ashamed of the gospel, they have no hope but have accepted defeat. One sad characteristic of ordinary people, which makes them stagnant in life is their refusal to accept the authority of the Word of God. The Word is indestructible; it cannot deny itself, it's quick and powerful. It's obviously devastating to hang around with ordinary people because they have no regard for the things of God. The Bible describes them as the simple. **Proverbs 22:3** says, *"the prudent man foreseeth the evil and hideth himself but the simple pass on and are punished"*. 'Punished' here, comes from the word 'suffer'. In other words, the simple pass on and suffer. They suffer because of negligence. King Saul suffered torment, he wallowed in fear, timidity, unrest. Though he was God's choice, he suffered because of his complacent attitude to the things of God **(1 Samuel 13-15).**

The simple man suffers for many reasons. The very first mistake he makes is regarding God's precious possession (themselves) as ordinary and acting so. This attitude of belittling God is an offence on its own. Stooping so low and trying to make the Word of God of non-effect is offensive. Defiling your body which is the temple of the living God is profane.

Living without regard for the things of God is opening the doors to suffering. Hence the simple man is tossed around by every wind of doctrine. He has no base, no specific local assembly he identifies with; he's just a Church inspector. The Bible says that the simple believes every word;

irrespective of where it's coming from. He believes every lie, fable, myth and tale; because he's not grounded in the truth.

Living In the Danger Zone

The danger zone is a darkness point of distraction, an unpleasant system which believers could drift into when they lose their sense of purpose. It's entering an area that's not in line with God's life which takes away their true identity. There are definitely consequences for living your life unregulated by the Word of God. When Christians blindly live their lives unregulated by God's Word, they stand open to the adversary.

Don't deceive yourself in believing you can steal, lie, be dishonest, hate or live on drugs, fornication, murder and claim to be in a right relationship with God. Even if you pretend to be a Saint, the Bible openly declares that friendship with the world is enmity with God.

We must make our salvation certain and open, not hidden, compromising or mingled with sin. Don't keep ungodly friends that draw you away from the presence of God.

It's important also not to deny your inner man the right environment to grow. Do you sing songs of unbelief? Do you look at pictures that deprive you of your dignity? Do you use unwholesome language or swear at people and yet go to Church at your convenience? This is certainly a danger zone for any Christian to tread.

A lukewarm Christian is endangering his life. The Bible reveals to us the mind of God on this matter in **Revelation 3:15,**

" I know thy works, that thou art neither cold nor hot: I would thou wert cold or hot. So then because thou art lukewarm, and neither cold nor hot, I will spue thee out of my mouth".

We carry the name of the Father, we are the expression of God's glory, carrying the radiance of God's divinity in humanity. Therefore our Heavenly Father expects the Word to have dominion over us, to rule our decisions, to guide our tongue, to control our daily affairs. The only way to live in God's realm is to stay in His Word, regardless of the affairs of this world. Don't let craze for money, promotion, health, children, fame, or other needs, deprive you of your true identity.

The most wonderful announcement is your Father possesses all these things. If you are in need of them, He says, ask and it shall be given unto you that your joy might be full **(John 16:24)**.

Seek first the kingdom of God and His righteousness; and all these things shall be added unto you. In other words, aim after doing things the *God way* and in His righteousness. Don't permit the world system to control you. Let the Word regulate your ways, thought and language. You are a child of God, live as one!

Expensive hobbies are depriving because they are wrongly placed, usually at the expense of the right habits. Set your priorities right. You can assess your spiritual accomplishments, assess your growth. How much time and value do you give to God?

Jesus always went into the wilderness to pray without distraction. This is to demonstrate the extent of the importance of separating oneself, entirely to God, without any distraction. I observed a certain brother who always arrived late to church, and his excuse was always that he was tired. One day I called him to find out if he was alright, or if he was doing late night jobs. I was shocked when he admitted it was his hobby that kept him up at night, as late as 4.00 am. He said he loved watching late night movies. That hobby was destroying his relationship with God, and he didn't know it. It was consuming his precious time. That was expensive indeed!

The danger zone is a wretched, miserable, poor, blind state. The book of Revelation describes this condition. *"Because thou sayest, I am rich, and increase with goods and have need of nothing; and knowest not that thou art wretched, miserable and blind"*. It's terrible to be in this condition, a poor spiritual state without realizing it.

Wonderful Christians

A Christian should not take the Word out of context, arguing blindly and trying to convince others around him to accept a selfish opinion. The Bible strictly warns against this attitude, Paul started by saying to the Galatians, ***" I marvel that you are so soon removed from him that called you into the grace of Christ unto another gospel... As we said before, so say I now again, If anyone man preach another gospel unto you, let him be accursed".*****(Galatians 1:6,9)**

If this matter was not taken lightly by Paul,

we as believers must come to terms with what the gospel implies, and what we believe. The gospel is the power of God unto salvation to every one who believes it, to the Jews first and then to the Gentiles. The Word of God is the life carrying faculty of God, so the gospel put in words, is the power of God to make His life manifest in a man. Not by man paying for it, not by merits, but by God's grace.

Galatians 2:16 says, ***"knowing that a man is not justified by the works of the law, but by the faith of Jesus Christ ..."***

The gospel simply means good news; that the life which we now live in the flesh, we live by the faith of the Son of God, who loved us and gave Himself for us. It's wonderful that we can live our lives by the faith of God, no longer controlled by the flesh, lust, or enslaved by the senses. We are now controlled by the Word. As much as we permit God's Word to regulate us, we must not overlook the fact that we are the light of the world, we are pacesetters and everyone who looks at us obviously observes God.

But we can misrepresent our Heavenly Father by refusing to grow unto maturity. For example, praying at the wrong time or not paying attention; busy constructing a letter to your lecturer, intending to win him to Christ, while a lecture is going on. He would probably end up being careful of you!

Christians are the most productive workers a man can employ. The Bible declares whatever they lay their hands to do shall prosper **(Psalm 1:3)**. I'm referring to believers who make the Word a priority. The Bible declares that *"whosoever looketh into the perfect law of liberty and continueth therein, he being not a forgetful hearer shall be blessed in his deeds"* **(James 1:25).** The Bible admonishes us to mind our business. The attention you place on issues related to you should be with the wisdom of God's Word.

A wise man is one that applies the wisdom he has. *"Who is a wise man and endued with knowledge among you? Let him show out of a good conversation his works with meekness of wisdom."* **(James 3:13)**. You must have good works to present because these works will be tried by fire. The coming of Jesus should not put fear or guilt in the heart of a believer but confident assurance of a glorious union with him. You must take your salvation more seriously, not a Church *'sleeping beauty'*, whose eyes and ears take a break, as soon as the Word comes.

Pathetically some Christians who are very involved in church, pay more attention to moving around, just observing, just working even at odd times, they pay more attention to work at the expense of the Word, it's time to set priorities right.

Many people face extreme difficulty in having a successful, life-long relationship with their spouse, friends and family. Life is more fulfilling when you are in the midst of loving and caring people. You are at your best at work and home, when surrounded by people with a 'warm spirit'; people without evil intentions, suspicions, or misinterpretations. The most enriching life is highlighted in **Galatians 5:22-23**

"But the fruit of the spirit is love, joy, peace, longsuffering, gentleness, goodness, faith,
"Meekness temperance: against such there is no law."

The nature of every believer is love, since that is the nature of God. Anything short of love is contrary to God's way of life. This nature is not carnal, hence the Bible says in **Romans 5:5,**

"And hope maketh not ashamed; because the love of God is shed abroad in our hearts by the Holy

Ghost."

This is the evidence of a Spirit-filled man of God. Unfortunately, there are too many carnal believers who only love those that love them, but what differentiates a believer from the world is his in-depth nature of love causing him to love all men.

The simple fact about living happily with people is seen in your expressions. Your expression reveals your reaction, either pleasure or displeasure. Your expression can be hidden or blown open. However, it exposes itself with time. It's what some people refer to as *'How I feel'* or *'my feelings'*.

As a result of these carnal-induced phrases, many cases have been taken for granted because some people just expressed their feelings over a matter considered offensive or embarrassing. Sometimes, these cases are blown out of proportion and if you're quick at reacting, you might find yourself on the defensive, always apologizing for misunderstanding comments, because you exposed yourself to listening to just anything.

Some folks have been frustrated in their places of work, because they have a personal self-concluded impression of been overworked, taken for granted or considered insignificant. There are either two things to be done: work harder or butt out; keep away. These could help point you to the solution (self- check):

- ✓ How is my attitude in this regard? Am I over-reacting, nervous or impatient?
- ✓ Do I take to corrections or detest them?
- ✓ Am I too proud to be authorized?
- ✓ Do I follow instructions, or prefer to have things my way?
- ✓ Am I better than my superiors?
- ✓ Am I disciplined to work effectively and glad to take to corrections?
- ✓ Do I respond to corrections immediately?
- ✓ Do I ponder over a lot of words till it makes me feel sorry for myself?

Note that every suggestion does not have to come from you. Every name mentioned does not have to be your name. If you specialise in bringing up people, you will realize by re-echoing their suggestions and making them feel important, you have done yourself a favor in raising your statutes. Jesus grew in wisdom and stature, and in favor with God and man by preaching the gospel to the poor, laying hands on the sick and afflicted, setting captives free, making people happy. The Bible declares in the book of Luke,

***"And Jesus increased in wisdom and stature, and in favour with God and man"*(Luke 2:52).**

Overlook the hurtful words, and let them be converted into encouraging words. Overlook the threat, and see it as a reward of imminent promotion, because God looks at your heart. If your boss is trying to abuse you, it's time to speak forth the word of God concerning your boss with boldness. Pray for a change in him and for yourself, pray for a better move. Let God take control. You can never lose your job. If your boss threatens to sack you because you refuse to have an affair with him, no problem. You did not lose your job, they lost you. Head on for a better job. You are in control.

Apply the Love Principle

You can change your relationships for the better if you apply the love principle. It worked for God, it will work for you. Whether it's your aggressive in-law, your uncooperative brother or sister, love will make you hear their voice differently, it will make you view their actions and motives differently. Take control of the relationship with patience, and see their helpless souls with a new passion. Your strength comes out as you remain unmoved by their words, because they cannot hurt you. You're untouched by their actions, because they have no effect on you. God stands strong on behalf of His children.

You can have a good relationship with people. There are a number of guidelines people can give you for developing good relationships such as remembering names, keeping a kind smile, giving honest compliments, being prepared to listen to people, and never arguing but supporting their views. These tips are good, but they have their limitations. The Bible says,

"There is a spirit in man: and the inspiration of the Almighty giveth them understanding" **(Job 32:8).**

Wisdom is the principal thing. The man with an excellent spirit will do everything in line with the nature of God, not to impress, but because it's his nature to do right. He is the righteousness of God in Christ Jesus **(2 Corinthians 5:21)**.

Quite a number of people have great problems in communicating. Maybe in spite of tips and guidelines taught on communication you still experience difficulty in effectively communicating with your listeners. To communicate effectively, your words must come from your inner most being; for out of your inward part shall flow rivers of living waters Then your words will not be selfish but kind, not self-centred but considerate. Your smile will be encouraging; filled with life. That is the actual purpose of communication.

Another translation for Communication is *'Koinonia'*, meaning *'Fellowship'*.

"But to do good and to communicate forget not: for with such sacrifices God is well pleased."**(Hebrews 13:16)**

In other words, God is pleaed with the fellowship or communication of believers. Our communication brings edification to the hearer. The real life will communicate to your heart. A man with a recreated spirit talks from the innermost part of his being. His words create impact, portray the virtues of God's Spirit and bring edification to his listeners. God honors his words.

Therefore, if the secret of a successful relationship borders around effective communication, it means that you are designed to prosper in this area because the words that now come out of your mouth are spirit and life. They are not mere words, but active, operative, energizing and effective, full of power to win and for results.You will touch your hearers.They will desire your words like the people that followed our Lord Jesus just to hear Him speak. No man ever spoke like Him, the people stayed with Him for three days without food, just to hear Him speak. How wonderful!

Don't Lay Blames!

Blaming your father or mother or an acquaintance for your misfortune is responding to a lie from the pit of Hell. When you realise that no one can dictate your destiny but you and God, you will live a new kind of life. When you make His Word a priority, He would direct your path. In other words, give Him a free course to direct all your affairs. Don't waste your precious time blaming someone for any misfortune in your life. Whether someone wronged you or not, God will restore your wasted years. He would redeem your years in fruitful measures.

Think the best thoughts about others, see the best in others, and believe that if you can be kind, and walk in love, others can do the same. If you've made mistakes, relax. God has just started a new thing, to turn these mistakes, for development.

"Be ye therefore followers of God as dear children: And walk in love, as Christ also hath loved us and hath given himself for us as an offering and a sacrifice to God for a sweetsmelling savour." **(Ephesians 5: 1-2)**

You can forget the losses and the hurts. Start afresh. Don't put yourself in a vacuum. Don't wallow in ignorance and enjoy it. Everyone wants to be identified with success, square your shoulders because you are a bundle of success.

Some attitudes are rampant today: children running away from home simply because they refuse to be controlled by their parents. Christians moving from Church to Church, evidently as a result of wanting to have their own way. There is no discipline over their appetite. We have to train ourselves and rule our hearts with the Word of God. Renew your mind with the Word daily.

When people believe they have an option they can afford to takes things for granted. Careless talks, expensive jokes, inconvenient jesting, mockery should never be associated with a believer. As little as they seem, the Spirit of God detests them. They rob you of your true nature; they destroy your personality and belittle you. As a matter of fact, let it never be in the life of an anointed vessel of God like you!

"Let all bitterness, and wrath, and anger,and clamour, and evil speaking, be put away from you, with all malice: And be ye kind one to another, tenderhearted, forgiving one another, even as God for Christ's sake hath forgiven you." **(Ephesians 4:31)**

Frustrated Marriages

Most marital problems are usually planted during courtship. Your courtship to a large extent determines the kind of marriage you're preparing for. It's either a godly marriage or a compromising marriage. Some Christian folks only please their spouses at God's expense. They leave Church in spite of what their Pastors advise because they feel offended. Some people even get married irrespective of their Pastor's, parents' and brethren's advice. I will encourage you to reflect over the past, as you encounter the present.

***"Correction is grievous unto him that forsaketh the way: and he that hateth reproof shall die."* (Proverbs 15: 10).**

It's what you sow you will reap. It's an unchanging law. You have to destroy what you've sown by going to the root, because the foundation of life is in the root. This means you don't deal with a situation from the physical view point in life.

Being loose and wanting your own way irrespective of what the Word of God says, is an act of indiscipline which eventually leads to a great deal of disappointments. The Bible says,

***"Mortify therefore your members which are upon the earth; fornication, uncleaness, inordinate affection, evil concupiscence, and covetousness, which is idolatory."*(Colossians 3:5)**

Give yourself sound training. Don't compromise your righteousness. The Bible boldly instructs us to mortify our members. In other words, we are to put to death the things of the flesh (Romans 8:13). Prospective partners should appreciate courtship as a training ground. A relationship set with a vision and purpose, approached on God's principles, with such solid foundation is programmed to succeed. Seek to have a home whose builder and maker is God. How much respect do we have for our vows made on the altar before God? **(Isaiah19:21)** Are they forgotten over time or were they just recited at the altar. Your marriage should not be built on helpless confessions, submitting to fate, for better and for worse, in poverty and in wealth, in sickness and in health. There is a faith life profession of vows that grooms you from the onset to set your marriage on the Word. The bridegroom is enjoined to love his bride as Christ loves the Church, and the bride to respect her husband; to stand in the faith of the gospel of our Lord Jesus Christ in health, prosperity and joy.

Follow after what is real. What you see, feel and hear as long as it is inconsisitent with the Word of God is not real **(2 Corinthians 4:18).** Look unto Jesus and not unto your spouse and He will perfect your marriage and all that concern you.

Don't Take This For Granted

You might have shared an apartment with someone whom you believed used you. Probably you did not approve of his way of life or the way his kids were brought up, or their non-challant attitude. Whenever you refer to an experience you had with an acquaintance while he was sharing his home with you, irrespective of his behavior, I always want you to remember the first day he took you into his house. It must have been a testimony for you to have shelter. Think again about how you desperately needed his help and how he offered you assistance. Remember that your response was *'Thank you'*. In spite of any circumstance, remember that you are there to set examples not to depend on them, because God is your source. You are there to represent Christ, to express His love, and not to complain. You are there to pray for them, and show that you appreciate them. Jesus honours our appreciation **(Colossians 3:15).**

Don't ever take things for granted. Contribute positively to the well-being of the people around you. It's a legacy you will always be remembered for.

A kind person is not a fool, though the

world may think so. The world claims others will take advantage of a kind person or suggests the kindness is an ulterior motive, or that he would eventually regret his unnecessary kind nature. Kindness is a spiritual fruit. It's not done in exchange for a reward, or announced openly. This is why it's a struggle for the flesh to give. But a spirit-controlled man knows that it's a way of life. He knows giving opens the gateway to receiving.

Your Conversation

One day, record a visitor who speaks unruly on a tape. After he is gone, listen to your conversation. Then, notice carefully your contributions. Assess yourself with the following: supportive, indifferent, quiet, correcting or inspiring? Always remember that your silence means consent in communication.

Some people are so used to criticizing their countrymen and government, that in their subconscious they do the same, but thank God for His Word that has taught us to be prayerful over the affairs of our nation. Our confession must change towards those that are in office, hence influencing the course of our nation. The more we speak God's Word towards our nation, the more we put His Word into operation in the corridors of power.

If you've developed yourself over time to have itching ears, discussing the affairs of men and women you know, STOP! before it's too late. Make a deliberate decision to keep away from criticisms. It will definitely destroy you. Let your words concerning people be described as inspiring, motivating and encouraging.

"Let your speech be always with grace, seasoned with salt, that ye may know how ye ought to answer every man." **(Colossians 4:6)**

Listen To Your Heart

This is usually the advice the world can offer. Confiding in an unbeliever is a waste of time, the Bible declares that in the counsel of the godly there is power **(Proverbs 11:14)**. You can only listen to your heart if you have the right counsel stored up in it. Intense frustration has led many to make wrong decisions and sometimes confusion suppresses others to be irrational, irrespective of the Word. God is a master planner, He directs your path effortlessly, when you make Him your guardian. In a situation of desperate need don't cut off the Angel of His Presence. He is the Ancient of days working ahead and on behalf of His children, especially at a time when the situation appears at its worst. When you trust entirely in your Heavenly Father, He would do exceedingly abundantly above all you can ever think or imagine.

In a situation of desperate need, the Angel of God's presence always wants to take full control. This is the right time for God to prove Himself in the patience of His children. Many react too fast and refuse to respond to the Word. The secret is your response; ***'look into the perfect law of liberty and continue therein'***. Don't look at the world, but look at the Word of God.

"Because thou hast made the LORD, which is my refuge even the most High, thy habitation; There shall no evil befall thee, neither shall any plague come nigh thy dwelling. For he shall give his angels charge over thee, to keep thee in all thy ways."
(Psalm 91:9-11)

Just Start!

Someone is wondering, *"When will I ever fulfil my dreams, my ambitions of going to the university?"* Have you ever come across a messenger in a firm, who became a typist, advanced as a secretary, a legal practitioner and eventually rose to be the managing director of the firm? How much more a child of God, if God dwells in you? You have the ability to cause a change. Always remember that if God be for you no one can be against you **(Romans 8:31)**. In other words no one can defeat you. Start living your dreams today. The Word of God says ***"He giveth power to the faint; and to them that have no might he increaseth strength."*** **(Isaiah 40:29).**

4

Where is your Self-esteem?

How you treat yourself is of great importance to God. Your body, soul and spirit are all relevant functional parts of you, considered to be very important to your Heavenly Father. The Bible reveals this in **1 Corinthians 6:19-20**,

"Know ye not that your body is the temple of the Holy Ghost which is in you, which ye have of God, and ye are not your own? For ye are bought with a price: therefore glorify God in your body, and in your spirit, which are God's."

You are not your own anymore, you're God's. He bought you with an expensive price, and expects you to value His precious possession, which is you. He doesn't want you to look down on yourself. You are God's masterpiece. Carry yourself with dignity, as one in whom the Spirit of God dwells **(1 Corinthians 3:16).**

Some people have very low self-esteem. This could be a constant inner battle for life, resulting in an identity crisis. One major reason for this is a lack of confidence in oneself, for obvious reasons, ranging from child abuse, verbal abuse, peer pressure, deprivation of all sorts to a lack of good education.

The good news is that as believers, we have the Greater One on the inside of us. Our confidence is not in our ability but in God's. We have His ability; His power invested in us. A low self-esteem has very detrimental implications. It has forced a number of people to commit suicide. Several have gone into drugs, prostitution and various crimes for the simple fact that life seemed too hard to cope with. They could not manage life on their own. They did not believe in themselves. They could not place any value on their lives.

Losing one's individuality is one thing, but putting up a facade to impress people is definitely breathing a lie all year round. No doubt, a lot of teenagers need help. They are in a very vulnerable situation. A mistake in their life, without the support of their parents, could amount to life-long problems. Youths living for Christ make a whole world of difference.

For a youth to display leadership traits very early in life, should take no one by surprise. You are a leader. The Bible describes how Jesus taught the Pharisees and Scribes at the temple. Your parents may not be your role models; thank God He has provided His Word and the Holy Ghost to teach you all things **(John 15:16).** He has given us mentors and spiritual leaders to counsel us and pray for us as well. God has great plans for you. He wants to train you and develop you for leadership. It only requires a submissive heart; one that does not struggle to do or have things his own way.

"The Lord doth build up Jerusalem: he gathereth together the outcasts of Israel.
"He healeth the broken in heart, and bindeth up their wounds. "**(Psalm 147:2-3)**

Let God build you. Let Him organize your affairs. Permit Him to work in every facet of your life. Then, He can have full hold over you without the risk of your falling prey to the enemy's tricks.

To be caught in the web of low self-esteem is the devil's channel of destroying a Christian. The constant haunt to disregard yourself, think nobody loves or cares for you would not contribute any positive impact to your life. Even if you are actually faced with your friends disserting you for someone probably, better than you. Maybe you took solace in keeping a stressful relationship with someone who made your life miserable, someone who could not accept your friends or your family complained about everything you did, wanted to change your clothes or make up, even monitored your movement, obviously a pressure relationship. In similar circumstances some women have killed their children because they wanted to keep a successful relationship with a selfish friend. I wonder if they considered the fact that this friend could walk away at anytime, the same way their biological father did. You don't have to pressurize yourself, trying to impress someone to love you. The love of God is sure, His love for you is everlasting. Nothing will separate you from the love of God. God takes delight in His children, whom He created for His glory. The book of **Isaiah Chapter 43 verses 7** and **21** contain beautiful words from God about His children.

"Even every one that is called by my name: for I

have created him for my glory, I have formed him, yea, I have made him. This people have I formed for myself; they shall show forth my praise."

All that our God has created are in perfect condition and are for His pleasure. We bring God great pleasure when we value what He created. Starting from you, your brothers, sisters, friends etc.

When someone loves you, he goes out of his way to show it. He goes to the shop to select a nice gift for you. He thinks of your smile as he presents the gift to you. He imagines how nice you would look when you wear it. It's wonderful to be loved and happy. The Bible says *Happy is that people whose God is the LORD* **(Psalm 144:15).** They are admired simply because they are loved. Consider yourself blessed, having God's favour invoked upon you. David recognized and appreciated God's love for him, when he said, *"The Lord is my Shepherd "* **(Psalm 23: 1)**

Oh, if you hear the words that pour out of the heart of an appreciative child, you will fall in love with God. I always want my words to reflect the nature of my Father, what counts most is to be a channel of praise to God. A song writer said, "Why should I be discouraged why should the shadows come, why should my heart be lonely…"

If you have made God the Lord of your life, let Him be your number one. His eyes move to and fro the earth, to show Himself strong on behalf of those whose heart are set towards Him. You are God's number one priority. He says,

***"...I have called thee by thy name; thou art mine, when thou passeth through the waters, I will be with thee…* (Isaiah 43:1-2).**

Not only is God there for you, but with Him working on your behalf, nothing shall by any means hurt you.

You might have been the breadwinner of your family and enjoyed having control until you lost your job, and you have not found any suitable job ever since. It's making you frustrated and depressed to be at home all year round with dependants. You feel worthless, especially with the thought of your wife alone supporting the family financially.

There's something my husband always says, *'if you don't have a job, make one'*. The thinking that we need capital to start any business is erroneous. Success is more than capital. What you really need is an idea, faith, a strong drive, potential and the will to start off. When these are in place, you are ready for success. God will provide the capital. If you will let Him, the ideas will come as you pray. When you direct your interest to God, He would organize your plans. God will work with you in the area of your interest. Let your interest measure up with His Word. He will give you an idea on how to get the capital. He'll supply your needs according to His riches in glory by Christ Jesus **(Philippians 4:19)**. Our God is a Master planner, a perfect organiser, don't forget this truth, you can depend on Him.

You should not permit circumstances or people to determine your worth. It doesn't matter what anyone thinks of you. You cannot please man, no matter how hard you try. You can only please God. He looks at your heart; your intentions and covers you with His shield of love. He protects you, while others will expose you. He will guide you while others judge you. He will love you when others turn their back on you.

The Pharisees were a typical example of pressure to our Lord Jesus Christ. They were persistent at embarrassing Him, they refused to obey Him or learn anything. They had no regard for miracles, they were determined to terminate Him. They instigated lies against our Lord Jesus

Christ. But it did not change Him from being our Healer, our Caretaker, our Teacher. He said, *" I must go about my Father's business..."* **(Luke 2:49)**. The Bible declared how Jesus went about doing good and healing all that were oppressed of the devil **(Acts 10:38)**. The law was not master over Jesus. Jesus was Master over the law. The law did not stop Him from displaying the nature of the Father. If Jesus had gone through mockery, betrayal, lies, ingratitude and He still remained a Victor, that simply means God has designed you a victor **(Romans 7:38).** Mockery, unemployment, divorce, failure, health problems are not enough to destroy God's design. He breathed His life into you. He is at work in you. The Amplified Translation makes it clearer:

"For it is God who is all the while effectually at work in you [energizing and creating in you the power and desire] both to will and to work for His good pleasure and satisfaction and delight." **(Philippians 2:13).**

You're not alone in this world. These circumstances don't have the right to change your self- esteem. Don't allow anything to interfere with your relationship with God. You are God's will created for His pleasure, satisfaction and delight.

You might have heard some people say, *"This problem makes me unhappy and I cannot pray anymore."* You have the responsibility to make yourself happy. It's a big mistake to allow problems interfere with your prayers to God. That's how the devil tries to destroy a Christian. He steals the Word to destroy the believer. While he has your attention over one problem, he is paving way for more serious ones to come. As long as you are negligent of the Word, the devil can get your attention but God's Word has the supernatural ability to build you up. What you're going to be can only be determined by you. Change the way you view challenges, don't be afraid of things.

"No weapon that is formed against thee shall prosper; and every tongue that shall rise against thee in judgement thou shalt condemn. This is the heritage of the servants of the LORD and their righteousness is of me, saith the LORD." **(Isaiah 54:17)**

God has destined you for His glory. You have a role to play as His child. Discover it. No matter your occupation, God requires you to obtain fulfillment in the gospel.

Nobody would want to employ someone who comes for an interview begging for employment, because he's frustrated or unhappy. He's desperately in need of money, has no friends, is lonely and dislikes himself. You would rather help him financially but not employ him to work for you because you want someone who is charming, confident, honest, trustworthy, attracts customers, is hardworking and good at the job; not someone seeking sympathy, otherwise, he would wreck your business. An employer would pay a fortune to have a staff who loves smiling. Nobody enjoys a frowning face. It repels. The truth is you create a force field around you when you have a good self-esteem. You invite people like you, *"Like begets like."*

Don't be regulated by moods. This week you're happy, next week is a struggle. You have the nature of God. You're the righteousness of God in Christ. See yourself the way God sees you, not what you consider about yourself.

"Thou through thy commandments has made me wiser than my enemies: for they are ever with me. I have more understanding than all my teachers for thy testimonies are my meditation. I understand more than the ancients, because I keep thy precepts.

***I have refrained my feet from every evil way, that I might keep thy word."* (Psalm 119:98-101)**

Build yourself in the Word. Stop putting yourself down with your precious mouth. You're God's precious possession, worthy of the death of His only begotten Son. He became sin that you might become the righteousness of God in Him **(2 Corinthians 5:21)**. He became poor that you might become rich **(2 Corinthains 8:9)**. When these become meaningful to you, you will never listen or believe in the devil's lies. Don't accept wrong thoughts: when the devil tells you *'You're a failure', 'You will surely die', 'You can never have a child', 'Your health is at stake', 'That person does not like you...'*,the list is endless.

God is on your case. Create the environment for Him to work with you. Rejoice! The steps of the righteous are ordered of God. It's important that you love the Lord with a pure heart. If you love God you will definitely love to please Him and do His will. Then, you will treat yourself with more respect. You will value the price He paid to redeem you. The love of God has been shed abroad in your heart by the Holy Ghost **(Romans 5:5)**, spread it to those around you. Those who live in love never regret it.

It's time to dream big, you're identified with Christ. You have an identity, you're not 'just a teacher', 'just a dentist', 'just a Mum or Dad'. Your identity is established through what you are committed to. What are you committed to? Be committed to the things of God and His Word; things of eternal value.

You are worth more than many sparrows. Value eternal life. It's certain that you will never desire another when you truly have Christ.

5

Show Me A Hopeless Case

The definition of a hopeless case is one that needs to be addressed at this point. It's apparent that its definition differs from one person to another. Let me put it this way: do you know someone in a state of despair, rejection or even in a state of condemnation? Probably you have even been told a situation is incurable, irreparable, inconsolable or irrevocable. You are so desperate and confused because nothing within human imagination can alter the problem. Is that what you call a hopeless case?

I heard of a child, about five years of age, whose father just died at the time. After the funeral, she visited his grave. There by the graveside, she wept bitterly. Then, suddenly she said, *'Daddy, now that you are gone, who will take care of me; who will pay my school fees?'* That was one question nobody was ready to answer, but this child was desperate to know what the future held for her. Some businesses have collapsed, *'wrecked beyond repair.'* Some folks have been *'battered for life'* because of one misfortune or the other. Is that a hopeless case?

An incident in the Bible would have passed for a hopeless case, but by the time we're through looking at it, you would agree with me that God can turn any situation for your good.

Now journey with me to Pi-hahiroth by the Red Sea, as I revisit the scene of this great, indelible incident. Just before then, Pharaoh had pronounced the release of the children of Israel in the land of Egypt. However, on a second thought, he changed his mind concerning his decision, and planned to destroy them completely.

Pharaoh got six hundred of his choicest chariots with their captains and they pursued aggressively after the children of Israel.

When the children of Israel saw the Egyptian army on their chariots at close range, they were sore afraid. They cried unto the Lord and accused Moses of bringing them to the wilderness to kill them there. They were indeed shortsighted, because they had not known the kind of God they had in their camp.

"And Moses said unto the people, 'Fear ye not, stand still, and see the salvation of the LORD, which He will shew you to day: for the Egyptians whom ye have seen today, ye shall see them again no more for ever.
"The LORD shall fight for you, and you shall hold your peace.
"And the LORD said unto Moses, Wherefore criest thou unto me? <u>speak unto the Children of Israel, that they go forward:</u>
"But lift thou up thy rod, and stretch out thine hand over the sea, and divide it: and the children of Israel shall go on dry ground through the midst of the sea." **(Exodus 14:13-16)**

Moses was very desperate when he looked ahead of him and saw the Red Sea, knowing fully well that Pharaoh's army was approaching them from behind. He cried for help, then God ordered him to use *his rod,* for the solution was right there in his hands. When he responded to God's Word by stretching forth his hand, the rod split the great Red Sea into two and the children of Israel walked on dry ground across the Red Sea. Praise God.

What's in your hand? God can use whatever is in your hand, if you put your trust in him. It's not your cry, tears and suffering that move God, but how you exercise your authority in His Word. A child of God is not void of power and authority. He possesses the power of God unto salvation.

In other words, there is nothing like *'a hopeless situation'* in the vocabulary of God's children. Every child of God is an overcomer in this life. Every child of God is more than a conqueror; he is a victor! He's born into royalty. This is the essence of the gospel: to make available the power to live the good life.

End of The Road?

"Fire on the mountain? Run, run, run!": that is the usual solution for a troubled mind. In despair, complete helplessness, in trouble, debt, embarrassment, loneliness and shame. Go where nobody would talk about or laugh at you. Just quit, escape or disappear if you can. This could solve the problem, it would be the recommendation for man's search to overcoming devastating circumstances, whether self imposed or a 'natural' disaster.

If you've come to the end of the road, I have good news for you. When a believer comes to the end of the road, it only means a new road is just beginning. Jesus said clearly in **John 16:33,**

"In the world ye shall have tribulation: but be of good cheer, I have overcome the world.".

These words are mind-blowing."You have overcome the world". The Amplified Translation states it clearly,

"...in the world, you have tribulations and trials, distress and frustrations; but be of good cheer (take courage; be confident, certain, undaunted), for I have overcome the world. I have deprived it of the power to harm you and have conquered it for you)"

In other words, there is no power on earth that's capable of destroying the man who is backed by Deity. The power available to us is of two kinds. The first is *"Dunamis"*, which means the dynamic ability in you to cause changes, and *"Exousia"* that is, the delegated power or authority given to man by God. Jesus said,*"I have given you authority over all things."* That is to say, He has given you the power of attorney to use His Name, to change all forms of circumstances and situations. He said all power is given unto us in heaven and in earth **(Matthew 28:18).**

The good news is, He has made this power available to us, not to mope over what we have, but to use it. There will always be an occasion to use the power of God invested in a believer, unfortunately, the period when it should be utilised is usually the period when brethren either forget to use it, refuse to use it, or for one reason or the other do not use it.

Just before the ascension of our Lord Jesus Christ, he said in **Luke 24:49,**

"And behold, I send the promise of my Father upon you: but tarry ye in the city of Jerusalem, until ye be endued with power from on high".

This is serious information. You cannot afford to accept failure, it's not your portion, neither is it God's plan for you. Knowledge is vital. Once you locate the problem areas, the next step is to change it. Get ready for a change, it only takes your action.

A *'hopeless case'* is a state of the mind. When

you put your trust in God, you can never be disappointed. It's an established fact that neither tribulation, distress, persecution, famine, nakedness, peril nor sword can separate us from the love of God **(Romans 8:38-39)**. Whatever you're going through in life, you're not alone; the Greater One is in you. In other words, you can do all things through Christ who strengthens you. God will not fold His arms to watch you roam around in frustration. He covers you with His shield of favour. You're the only one that can fold your arms from receiving His love. God is always giving. You must be persuaded that,

"...neither death, nor life, nor angels, nor principalities, nor powers, nor things present, nor things to come,
"Nor height, nor depth, nor any other creature, shall be able to separate you from the love of God."
(Romans 8:38,39)

Hope Is Not Enough!

"And hope maketh not ashamed; because the love of God is shed abroad in our hearts by the Holy Ghost which is given unto us."**(Romans 5:5)**

The hope that always produces result is the one that has its roots in God. No man should hope in himself, for there is no strength in such hope. To hope in God is to trust entirely in Him for one's provision. Yet, hope is not enough to change circumstances until it is mixed with faith! Many Christians have hoped for changes in their jobs, finances, schools, homes and circumstances. And they're still hoping. A winner is one who lives above making statements like *'One day, it will work'* or *'Well, I hope everything will come out successfully.'* A winner announces that all is well because he knows that his expectation as a righteous man shall be met **(Proverbs 24:14).** He has such profound assurance in God's ability that he confidently declares it. While hope is the ingredient that makes you apply faith, faith is the response of the human spirit to the Word of God.

Believe what the Word says about you and as a result of your belief, act on it. Do not swallow any belief or surrender to any circumstance that is not in conformity with God's plan and purpose for your life. You must be responsive to the Word of God *as though your life depends on it* – the truth is it really does depend on it. Desist from making remarks that are not consistent with the plans, purpose and provisions of God. Remarks like *'I don't need to look for any job since there are no jobs available'* are not in line with God's Word. There is certainly a place specifically prepared for you. Ask before you judge yourself wrongly, then you will learn to appreciate God as a rewarder of those that diligently seek Him. The fact is that some folks don't find out until it's too late. You must find out what belongs to you in His Word. This way you build up your faith to receive from Him. If you don't ask in faith, even though He has all things, you can't receive.

***"But without faith it is impossible to please and be satisfactory to Him. For whoever would come near to God must [necessary] believe that God exists and that He is a rewarder of those that diligently seek Him [out]"* (Hebrews 11:6 ~ The Amplified Translation)**

***"Hitherto have ye asked nothing in my name; ask and ye shall receive, that your joy may be full."* (John 16:24)**

James 1:17 also declares that ***every good gift and every perfect gift is from above, and cometh down from the Father of lights, with whom is no variableness, neither shadow of turning.***

Our television programmes are really incredible. It is nothing but the hand of God. Countless millions have been greatly blessed by them. One of them, an inspirational one, *'Atmosphere for Miracles'* is quite awesome. We have received thousands of letters testifying to the awesome healing power of God transferred through the agency of TV sets to homes, causing healing of the body and setting people free.

There's one inspiring testimony I would like to share with you. It's the testimony of an aged woman and her son. Apparently the son had been watching *'Atmosphere for Miracles'* for quite some time before then. When he heard the doctor's report on his mother's case, he persuaded his mother to watch the programme too. His mother was having a complicated pregnancy and the doctor's report spelt death in every direction: the death of the child was certain while the mother may live or die. So pathetic.

However, during the course of the TV programme, after making sure that his mother was watching, the son entered the bathroom to take a shower. He said that a couple of minutes after entering the bathroom, he heard a loud scream, he dashed out and behold, it was his mother on the floor and right in front of her was a new born baby crying in a pool of blood. Hallelujah!

His mother later narrated that during the course of the programme, the minister, Pastor Chris told the viewers to stretch their hands towards the screen just before he prayed for them. She said, she moved toward the TV set and embraced it instead. While the prayer was on, she felt the power of God move on her body and she started having contractions in her abdominal region. And just before she knew what was happening, she had given birth. Praise God! This is not just a story, it is God at work on our behalf.

God establishes a blood covenant with anyone that believes in Him and declares Him as his Lord. Such individuals are His sons and daughters by right and by knowledge. I want you to note that when a family cuts a blood covenant with another, the family does not only partake of the strengths and weaknesses, blessings and curses of the other, but the members of the weaker family also take up the status of the firstborn of the stronger or richer one in all ramifications. They are said to have the right of the first born.

A Christian is one who is in a covenant relationship with God. God gave birth to Jesus through the agency of His Word by the Holy Ghost. Jesus Christ is His Firstborn **(Colossians 1:15,18),** and by virtue of your covenant with God, you now belong to the class of Jesus Christ. You have taken up the rank and fullness of Jesus Christ in nature, strength and wealth. You are no more a stranger but a (firstborn) member of His family:

"Wherefore remember, that ye being in time past Gentiles in the flesh, who are called Uncircumcision by that which is called the Circumcision in the flesh made by hands;
"That at that time ye were without Christ, being aliens from the commonwealth of Israel, and strangers from the covenants of promise, having no hope, and without God in the world:
"But now in Christ Jesus ye who sometimes were far off are made nigh by the blood of Christ.
"For he is our peace, who hath made both one, and hath broken down the middle wall of partition between us;
"Having abolished in his flesh the enmity, even the law of commandments contained in ordinances; for to make in himself of twain one new man, so making peace;" **(Ephesians 2:11-15).**

He lives and abides in us, not for a season, but forever. The middle wall of religious beliefs and worldly philosophies has been pulled down.

Now you have access to Him and He to you. There is a fellowship; an exchange of substances between you and Him. Remember that with God there is *no variableness, neither shadow of turning* **(James 1:17)**. How great is our God - from everlasting to everlasting, He is God and His Word concerning us remains the same. God never changes; the only things that change are the substances and situations to which His Word is applied. In other words, God's Word will bring a change to failure, defeat, sickness, discouragement, poverty, ignorance and the like.

Discover What's In Your Hands

You can succeed. You can make it no matter which situation you are in. Christ already made you a bundle of success when He rose from the dead. Since you believed in Jesus Christ as your Lord and Saviour, you entered into a covenant relationship with Him. As a covenant partner, you have the whole world **(1 Corinthians 3:21-22)** and all that is in it are at your beck and call. You are a success on every count.

"Know ye not that ye are the temple of God, and

that the Spirit of God dwelleth in you?
"If any man defile the temple of God, him shall God destroy; for the temple of God is holy, which temple ye are.
"Let no man deceive himself. If any man among you seemeth to be wise in this world, let him become a fool, that he may be wise.
"For the wisdom of this world is foolishness with God. For it is written, he taketh the wise in their own craftiness.
"And again, The Lord knoweth the thoughts of the wise that they are vain.
"Therefore let no man glory in men. For all things are yours;
"Whether Paul, or Apollos or Cephas, or the world, or life or death, or things present, or things to come, all are yours;
"And ye are Christ's; and Christ is God's."
(1 Corinthians 3:16-23).

All things are yours and they are in your hands. Success is in your hands. What you do with it is what matters now. This is your responsibility. What you make out of what is in your hand is what you vitally become in life. Let's have a look at God's way of living in this reality.

"This book of the law shall not depart out of your mouth, but you shall meditate on it [mutter, reflect on, speak to yourself] day and night, that you may observe and do according to all that is written in it. For then you shall make your way prosperous, and then you shall deal wisely and have good success." **(Joshua 1:8 ~ paraphrased)**

As you spend time to study God's Word you receive divine information on the plan and purposes of God for your life. Make a practice of reflecting on the Word, speaking it to yourself as though you are reminding or teaching yourself. Have you ever rubbed menthol on any part of your body? If it was rigorously done, apart from the sensation that came with the menthol, that part of the body would have also experienced a burning sensation. Reflecting on God's Word could be likened to that experience. In essence, when you meditate on God's Word, you're rubbing it onto your human spirit till it sinks into it. At that moment when the reality of God's Word dawns on your spirit, you receive revelation knowledge. These stored pieces of information are what you live by; they regulate your speech, attitudes, actions and reactions to life's situations. You speak them, and act them in real life.

God's Word contains the ingredient to live successfully in life: counsels, admonitions, reproofs, and instructions on how to deal wisely in life. Reflect on it at all times and then you will speak success, demonstrate success habits and attitudes and have good success in all spheres of life: at your new job, in handling your finances, in managing your home, at handling your responsibilities, in your organisation, in your speech and all your endeavors. If you don't have a job, make one; start by doing what you enjoy most, which is of benefit to others, then your job would be a great pleasure to you. Therefore,

"Let the saints be joyful in glory: let them sing aloud upon their beds. Let the high praises of God be in their mouth, and a two-edged sword in their hand;" **(Psalm 149:5-6)**

Take joy in what He has done. Take joy in what He can do, and what He's about to do. Protect yourself with the Sword of the Spirit, which is the Word of God. It will drive sickness away from you. It will provide for your life, and establish you in righteousness.

You must sit back and stop worrying. Worry deprives you of all that God has in store for you. It's a deceptive sin that renders God's Word of non-effect. It is *faith* that is exercised in the *ability* of the defeated adversary – the devil. If you want a change, dwell on the reproductive power of God's Word.

***"...Who, by (in consequence of) the [action of his] power that is at work within us, is able to [carry out His purpose and] do superabundantly, far over and above all that we [dare] ask or think [indefinitely beyond our highest prayers, desires, thoughts, hopes, or dreams]"* (Ephesians 3:20 ~ The Amplified Translation).**

So you must not allow yourself to worry. Forget about what happened in the past and the mistakes of the past. Neither should you be anxious about your future. Focus on all that you do today. Today is the connection to the future you long for. You're a bundle of success going somewhere to *'happen'*. So don't just exist, depending on luck to take charge. The Greater one indwells you. When you're in control, you create the right enviroment for God to work. However, looking down on yourself and speaking negative words tie God's hands. He that is in you is greater than he that is in the world **(1 John 4:4).** Let Him talk through you and act through you. There will never be a dull moment for you, just be the one *'happening'*.

6

A Fresh Move

***"And you hath he quickened, who were dead in trespasses and sins;"* (Ephesians 2:1)**

We have been quickened together with Christ; we have been made alive. Christ has made everything you will ever require for living available. Don't give up on yourself. No one can write you off, if anyone does, he's in for a surprise because God takes over from where man's efforts fail. God never writes anyone off, He prepares men for changes. Just let it dawn on you that you are not your own anymore, you are God's;

"What? Know ye not that your body is the temple

of the Holy Ghost which is in you, which ye have of God, and ye are not your own?
"For ye are bought with a price: therefore glorify God in your body, and in your spirit, which are God's." **(1 Corinthians 6:19,20)**

You're now a new man in Christ (2 Corinthians 5:17). The moment you put on Christ, you began your walk in the newness of the Spirit beyond the flesh, which is life at God's capacity – a life that can never fail. Let nothing hinder your progress, especially when all hope seems dashed because even then, God proves Himself. Jesus said to Paul the Apostle about 2000 years ago and still says to you today,

"...My grace is sufficient for thee: for my strength is made perfect in weakness. Most gladly therefore will I rather glory in my infirmities, that the power of Christ may rest upon me." **(2 Corinthians 12:9)**

As you rest your heart on God's Word, the power of Christ will rest on you. Instead of packing your bags, relax and establish an intimate relationship with God. When your relationship with God is good, it will certainly make a world of difference in your home, job, and even in the Household of God.

A Visit to the Life-giving Faculty

The Word of God is the life-giving faculty of the Godhead. It's the only entity that all things obey: whether animate or inanimate, ugly circumstances or *'irrevocable'* situations, the Word of God is the Head over all things;

"For by him were all things created, that are in heaven, and that are in earth, visible and invisible, whether they be thrones, or dominions, or principalities, or powers: all things were created by him, and for him:
***"And he is before all things, and by him all things consist."* (Colossians 1:16,17)**

The Word of God carries along with it the active power of God, which has the transforming ability to cause changes in anything in accordance to the plans, purposes and provisions of God.

"So shall My word be that goes forth out of My mouth: it shall not return to Me void [without producing any effect, useless], but it shall accomplish

that which I please and purpose, and it shall prosper in the thing for which I sent it." **(Isaiah 55:11 ~ The Amplified Translation)**

"Through faith we understand that the worlds were framed by the word of God, so that things which are seen were not made of things which do appear. **(Hebrews11: 3)**

"The earth was without form and an empty waste, and darkness was upon the face of the very great deep. The Spirit of God was moving (hovering, brooding) over the face of the waters. And God said, Let there be light; and there was light." **(Genesis 1:2-3 ~ The Amplified Translation).**

It was the spoken Word of God that birthed every creation on earth today. In the same way, every circumstance came into being with time, as a result of words spoken, whether evil or good. The Bible also says,

"Of his own will begat He us with the word of truth, that we should be a kind of firstfruits of his creatures." **(James 1:18)**

We are the firstfruits of His creatures. We

are His seed set to prolong His reign **(Isaiah 53:10)**. God has made us winners and not quitters! A winner is one that comes out victorious in a battle, from a problem, from a mistake. Having faced several challenges, the victor refuses to give up until he becomes a master over such circumstances. As a believer, you are a "ready-made" winner. Even if you had fallen or failed at one time or the other, acknowledge who you are and come out victorious. This attitude would conquer doubts or an indifferent response, once you chin up to proclaim this scripture.

***"...in all these things we are more than conquerors through Him that loved us."* (Romans 8:37)**

So, don't give up on your present challenge, don't resign from your job, because your boss dislikes you. How are you sure your next boss will like you? He could be worse than the first. Don't give up on your relationship or marriage. Don't give up on you! Quit running! For how long will you run? It's better to win in your place of work; then, you could opt for another job. Don't leave out of frustration, but because you have reigned, you have conquered and you need another place to manifest His glory. Whenever you start a project – the building of a house, an educational course, a new job or any new endeavour, operate the partnership sequence, be sure to connect with your heavenly Father, your master organiser. Pay great attention to put God in His rightful position in vital issues that concern you. Speak His Word to your projects daily. Seek God's Word before executing a project, let Him guide your proposals and lead you with His wisdom. Everything you own also belongs to Him. Therefore, let Him be in charge. Don't only consult with Him when you are '*stuck*' and abandon Him when everything is '*rosy*'. If you want to start anything you want to finish, start with God first. You can only do it right the first time when you make His Word of utmost importance in your life. Seek His Word concerning whatever you're embarking on and do it exactly the Word way.

Some people have wondered whether God's Word is applicable to all issues man will ever encounter in life, be it great or small. The Word of God is a panacea: it provides solutions to all problems and answers every question.

Think again about it - this time think God's way! Packing your bags and leaving is not good enough. Don't run away from Church or from the ministry or from home or even from the country for any flimsy reason. If God had given up on you, you would have perished. But He didn't give up on you and never will. He is a God that overcomes; one that conquers. And since you have that same Spirit of God in you, know that you are as He is – an overcomer;

***"Ye are of God, little children and have overcome them: because greater is He that is in you, than he that is in the world."* (1 John 4:4)**

A Look Again through God's Binoculars

***"Blessed is the man that trusteth in the LORD and whose hope the Lord is."* (Jeremiah 17:7)**

When your relationship with your Father is established, you will definitely trust Him completely, without an element of doubt in your heart. Moreover, your confidence will be established as you fellowship with His Word. Let your focus be on your relationship with your Heavenly Father and not on the present problems. Remember victors call them challenges. Total focus on your challenges will distract and distabilise you. So don't focus on them, rather cast all your cares upon Jesus and be resolute to focus on God and His Word.

Whatever challenges are trying to drift you away from God must be handled decisively. Simply take the problem to God. Permit Him to change those things you cannot alter. But you have a role to play. Start by changing your confession from, *'How will I handle it, how will I cope with it, how will I pay my bills?'* to *'My God shall supply all my needs and take care of me.'* This definitely implies that you are in koinonia (fellowship) with your God. Since no case is hopeless with God, certainly no case is hopeless with you. But you must change your attitude to unpleasant situations, since it's not the problem that counts but your attitude towards it. Consider every problem a challenge to prove your level of maturity.

Determination

In one of our recent 2-day outreach programmes, a lady came limping to one of our meetings. While my husband, Pastor Chris, was ministering, this lady walked straight up to give her testimony. She was a beautiful lady in her early seventies. She said when she witnessed all the great miracles that had been happening to people in the congregation, her faith rose. She had been in great pains for years; she could hardly lift up things. She struggled to walk. She was drawing the sympathy of many people; friends and family. She said she was tired of sympathy and human help. She figured that if God could do all the miracles she had witnessed for many people with similar problems that day, He could do the same for her. '*I was determined that I would not go home without my miracle, there's no reason why I should not be healed because God is a healer'*, she said. While she was worshipping God during the course of that session, she noticed that the pain had left her body. She was totally healed. She boldly declared she was tired of her former state, she wanted her healing with strong determination. Truly, healing is the children's bread. It's for every believer to live in divine health.

The human spirit, which is the real you, is designed to respond to the Word of God. As you encourage yourself in the Lord by searching the scriptures and speaking the Word of God to yourself, your human spirit gets excited. God's Word is the escape route for every crisis in life.

Also note that God inhabits the praises of His people. As you praise the Lord and rejoice in the Lord, you create an atmosphere of miracles in your life.

"Thus saith the Lord GOD unto these bones; Behold, I will cause breath to enter into you, and ye shall live:

"And I will lay sinews upon you, and will bring up flesh upon you, and cover you with skin, and put breath in you, and ye shall live; and ye shall know that I am the LORD.

"So I prophesied as I was commanded: and as I prophesied, there was a noise, and behold a shaking, and the bones came together, bone to his bone. **(Ezekiel 37:5-7)**

Dry bones are a type of *'dead, irreparable'* situation. The Word of God is the life-giving faculty of God. As you speak God's Word to the situation, the life of God is imparted into it to come alive.

Are you getting discouraged because you have waited so long? Do you think God does not care anymore for you? Or are you amongst those who have been prayed for concerning your ailment but there seems to be no positive change in your condition? Or probably the doctor has adopted several therapies and everything is still the same? Child of God, don't despair; miracles are real! The *'Fourth man'* **(Daniel 3:25)** is still with you. You may not be able to see Him with your physical eyes, but know that Jehovah – the covenant keeping God, backs you up. Decide today never to allow any challenge drag you down, don't consider suicide or revenge. Instead of focusing on the problem, look up to Jesus; the Author anf Finisher of your faith. Call upon His Name and He would save you. Don't give up. Now is the time to apply all you have learnt and make changes for the best. Don't pack your bags yet!

**To know more about
the ministry and messages of
Pastors Chris & Anita Oyakhilome
contact:**

CHRIST EMBASSY

aka Believers' LoveWorld Inc.

LONDON ADDRESS:

Christ Embassy Int'l Office
Suite 219 Estuary House
Ballards Road
Dagenham RM10 9AB

P.O. Box 21520
London E10 5FG
Tel/Fax: -208-5172367

NIGERIA ADDRESS:

P.O. Box 13563,Ikeja,
Lagos, Nigeria.
Tel: 01-4934392-3; 7740109; 7740243

email:cec@christembassy.org.ng
website:www.christembassy.org

LoveWorld Publications & Tapes Ministry

Reaching out with the gospel,
Building up the saints,
With excellence and clarity.

Faith comes to you as you hear the Word of God. We recommend our books, video and audio tapes for your spiritual development.

The messages are designed to show you how to be fruitful and productive and cause faith to rise in your heart to do just that.

Get yours today and see a transformation in your life.

Books by Anita Oyakhilome

WISDOM FOR WOMEN

This timely book by Anita Oyakhilome contains timeless truths from the Word of God for the woman and the man desiring to be filled with the awesome treasures of wisdom for today's living.

UNENDING SPRING OF JOY

Life, they say, is full of ups and downs, and you cannot always be joyous. But hang on a minute, there is a new storyline which says you can have joy unspeakable and full of glory!

This joy comes from your inner man and is ever constant, irrespective of circumstances and situations of every day life.

Explore with Rev. Anita in this inspirational book as she shows you it is your choice to be joyful, and only then can the power of the gospel come alive in you.